Third Day

GREY GOWRIE was born in Dublin in 1939. Educated and professionally engaged in England and the USA, he made his home in Ireland until 1983 when he moved to the Welsh Marches. He taught English and American Literature at Harvard and University College London and in 1972, on publishing his first collection of poems, he exchanged an academic career for business and public life. He has been a company chairman, a Cabinet minister, Chairman of the Arts Council of England and Provost of the Royal College of Art. He is married to the German journalist Adelheid von der Schulenburg and is a Fellow of the Royal Society of Literature.

T0167437

GREY GOWRIE

Third Day

New and Selected Poems

CARCANET

First published in Great Britain in 2008 by
Carcanet Press Limited
Alliance House
Cross Street
Manchester M2 7AQ

A CIP catalogue record for this book is available from the British Library
ISBN 978 1 85754 966 9 (paper) / 978 1 85754 990 4 (cased)

The publisher acknowledges financial assistance from Arts Council England

Typeset by XL Publishing Services, Tiverton
Printed and bound in England by SRP Ltd, Exeter

Contents

Part One. *Sixties*

PART ONE
Sixties

Bourgeois culture is no longer capable of producing heroes. On the high-brow level it only produces characters who are embodied consolations for defeat, and on the lowbrow level it produces idols—stars, TV 'personalities', pin-ups. The function of the idol is the exact opposite to that of the hero. The idol is self-sufficient: the hero never is.

John Berger

Birthday Song

Listen: she has leapt
from the impeccable water
into an air where words
make the right sound for her
without worrying: heartless: for her entirely.

Where is love? morality?
Two by two they are twining
a wavelike arabesque
white as the vacant, turning
scallop that brought her here. They fix the horizon.

The world has become an ocean:
shoreless, but held together
by a girl whom stars put
out of reach of worldly weather.
The moon is a cold shield; her wars are still far away.

Sea wind, curtain her day
old, completed body
by playing tricks with her hair.
We have too much to bear
as it is. We have seen her. She will not let go of her prey.

Penelope

Dreaming he quite forgot his darling's nature.
Sleep came to him in spirals. Usually
each layer of sorrow leapt upon the other
(the dark he'd always found malevolent)
until he writhed or wept or dreamed that she
lay weeping by him. Tonight was different.

He was the captain of a ship exploring
islands of consciousness, the hemispheres
of sleep. His sea was empty when a mooring
swung into view and from it a shrill voice
begged him to land. He knew the voice was hers
but felt betrayed to see a nightmare's face.

And yet, although the face was horrible,
the drowned eyes matched the beauty of his own
in sleep, even this sleep; less terrible,
too, than the wastes around him were its features.
The tangled skin and broken columns of bone
pleaded how once they had been lovely creatures:

Penelope engraved in her own ruin.
Words sewn upon the little mouth they haunted
told her adventure until, dreaming, there came to him
the knowledge that a child who fought the tempest
of his despair must be the one he wanted.
She came aboard and soon they made the conquest

first of themselves, then seas they tamed together;
all the horizons, their limits like a pain
of logic to him; legendary weather
at whose divining topmost mizzens broke.
Wolves in the rigging whimpered under the rain
Pallas or someone sent, but, as he woke,

it was the eyes which hurt him, not the wet
slaver of loneliness he took for spray.
A groundswell trembled also. Throwing regret
behind like bedclothes for the beasts to savage,
Ulysses the dreamer met his day
without the solace of her night-time image.

Arabian

Looking for Damascus
we have flown over dry land.
A few clouds wake
our river memories.

Somewhere underneath
the Princess came
with camels, no doubt, and eunuchs,
looking for Damascus,

a husband, incense and a green garden
all to herself. But these were
the fabled, dusty
days before aeroplanes.

History has it
no one was allowed to see her
except black girls and the eunuch
of longest standing,

but does not say
if she succeeded,
whose tracks are patterns now
in the dry land.

Our Lebanese pilot
has no use for them:
since each in his own way
finds out Damascus,

maps and radar
will lead him where
St Paul needed visions
as we do—only

ours are literal and tug the eye
off re-enactment. The hot browns
and purples of the desert, the places where
all but flowers last a million years,

grant their peace and memory to humans
homing on Damascus. Clouds may
obscure our landing but rumour goes
it's raining over there.

Baucis

Very delicately the wings
fall, the pellets contain seed
and must rot before the earth gets it.
There is enough damp loam for a century
of accident and their parturition
needs little or no wind.
Spring is assured for the sycamores.

A notice forbids litter and says
Mr A.T. O'Gorman planted them
as a memorial to his wife in nineteen thirty-
five: a thought affecting all
who come to see the fall in north New York.
It is too quiet to know if the trees whisper.

For Brer

The child comes out into the tunnelled garden.
He has little to say but he says beautifully.
The trees are swinging for him, all their birds
caught by all their branches.

Nothing persuades him this is not the moment
for throwing himself into byres or a real ditch,
the lime thumb-deep in the soil; not even cats
nor the women whose threats and nervousness
peck at the home's disorder.

The wind will go down soon, the terse cats
busy themselves with birds. It's time for dredging
and tractors approach from north in platoons.
He veers back to his folk who make him learn
poem after poem.

Child, cultivate words against your wish.
How else shall the day be done, the day recaptured
when the whole garden was rapt and the good sun
found its inhabitants dancing?

Lady Day

Take your theology like tea,
        saucer it, let
            your mouth and the cup's rim
                scald themselves with tannin;
                    crack your lips,
and let the acid in.

Drink and recall
            childhood's Methodist women
                tilting their cups, each little finger vertical
                  against black lace.
                      The wrong fingers! The tea-drinkers' eyes
avid for Grace.

Hate them, recite the poem
            you wrote in your cups.
                'Give the bishops barbiturates!' you said, mixing
                  your denominations up.
                  Stanzas I hardly remember—
slurred, abrupt.

Give me my wish tomorrow
            and I will design
                a mirror to hand back your God song
                  faithfully, line by line,
                      since the lost features that wrote it are all
gone—moonshine.

Father's Story

He lay in a small tub, before breakfast,
and had no idea death was approaching.
Nor was there any reason why
it should: from a clear sky
patrolled: no raids for a week.
He turned the hot tap on so water ran
in cataracts down his knees, floating
the dark gland beneath.

He had a towel to hand and turned the pages
of Stendhal carefully, not getting them wet.
Skies fell—incendiaries, remote
bullets. From a shot water tower
water ran down, diluted
fire and *The Charterhouse of Parma*.

He was found quickly (it all seems
a long time ago now), the breath still
bubbling to the surface. His family kept the book
and were glad he died in comfort.
Out of a clear sky a negligent blast
sunk him; no time for a last
private act, the prayer for a clean death.

Postscript: History

My father's face, Thirties-ish, unafraid,
looks sidelong from the photo near my bed.
Brown hair improbably slicked, he has a smile
in black-and-white which I could wear as well
had I the colouring for it. But my gaze
shies like a horse from looking at the days
of point-to-points and appeasement, when the idea
of love chose my parents, Hitler's classic fear
of inferiority made him choose the Jews.
Life is obsessive, so I confuse
A.H. and P.H-R., the bones they built
or cindered with my bones. All Europe's fault
's reflected by the glass while in my head
nations go haywire in my parents' bed.

Oberland

An alpine spring
occurs on many levels, like the land.
This town falls on the lake. At evening swans
collect by the jetty restaurants, come aboard.
They glance in the water-glass, order their plumage
with serpentine dab-dabs of neck and bill
to wait the camera, like fashion models.
Click and they move away. But the camera misses
what later, haltingly, the eye records:
two worlds of blue and white: the mountain white
beyond, swan white and sky-in-water blue.

Masked swans congregate often at Brienz.
Blurred by too much light the season's prosy
without their movement to dissuade the eye
from climbing up—into a high world
where steam and ravens and another spring,
not burgeoning but falling, need no swans
to decorate the stillness as these do,
whose wings melt in the sun like blobs of snow.

Insect Others

Beautiful in a way the way flies
work together in pairs so unobtrusively
they camouflage the need of their collusion.
One feeds while the other
dances—not only their
matter of ritual, precedence at a feast
whose afters will be tasted a hundred miles
from here in damp brows and running noses.
Rather air's roomful has come alive
and fly appetite, radiant, aching as music,
reads into the curt non-musical buzz
an exact and temporary balance all its own:
the female at meat, the male dancing about her.

Prairie Wind

A stammering wind
unlatches gates, shutters
all the way east. The noise
is mournful as old
sacking, ghostly in the way
of human noises
imposed on beasts.
Franciscans grant apes
enjoy their cigarettes,
jam sessions, tea parties
and TV excursions;
they pray for the minds
of men who ordain them.
Late century nature
longs to reject
words, words
but the winds drive
cars and cattle
to shelter, as trapped by
the rhetoric of self-
knowledge as man.
A few constants
hold. The winds of God
still rattle with awe
believers' bones
to whom creation is
actual, incredible,
as a hurricane's blind eye.
This wind blows
through me until I feel
its brunt on my spine
and these words
are written for the wind
to take and drown in
its own music: strange
in an element free
as air it alters
the sound of the newly
damned, the caged dog.

A Chance World

i

They want your blood. Jet white
trails erase bits
of sky over trees, new
parkway. Resident

starlings twit people
riding from work
or walking toward
their cars. An expected

girl walks to you,
a parcel in her hand, what's left
of the sun in her hair. You
will break with them.

ii

The trees stand in their allowed
earth, several
exposed tendrils reach out
from the pavement in search of still

water: a vain commotion.
Their branches look young, artificial
and rise in the sky like
music: a trick of the light.

iii

Look at the new rain. It slants
left as you look at trees
from right angles—chiaroscuro
in evening light. Spring

is betrayed when so many
images disconnect
the imagination.
You must screen them before your eyes

rend you. What is harder
than a concept? Not stones
nor the exigent tools of a chance
world alive by menace.

Sixties

Anyway, the moths came into the story
in student rooms, in 1965;
an evening caught between love and adultery
and it was electric to be alive
except a war unfolding in the East
blundered, with the sound off, on a screen
that took the light and gave it back again,
lovemaker, in our patterns of unrest.
Mothwing and rotorblade—a world in love
at war; a shadowy wife; a husband scared
to face the music of the draft: who cared?
Half-a-life on and in another country
at nightfall it is hard not to believe
the world, and we, turned out as we feared.

Outside Biba's

Flowers after rare rain, boutiques
sprout behind glass in our macadam city
and everyone's talking fashion.

A girl goes by
who must be unmarried but looks so marriageable
her dress is a hurricane of confetti
blown to her from someone else's wedding.

Think of the great skirts of childhood's women,
the New Look that swept the war away ...

No war now, no one poor under thirty,
all the Cold War babies dressed to kill.

Marion's Time

We made a slatternly congress
of two: up to our arms
and miracle hair in love.
Just seventeen, you wore
sexual precociousness like a Sunday suit
and I, hamfistedly
tender, hardly knowing what to do,
knew where to look.

Two months a mother,
with the baby already given away
to an adoption society, you came
down Elm Street at 8 a.m.
and blew into my room.
I was half-asleep
when you went about love.

That must have been about eight or nine years ago.

I married the English
cousin I told you about
and you got your Afro-American Ph.D.
In the photograph I see
your 'integrated' wedding shake like the bridal veil
you sighed for. Does the lift of veins
on the back of men's hands enchant you still?

You look happy. I heard all this lately.

I will not see you again.

The Last Local Ones

The pale stink of the Star Insurance Co.
offices drove a man down to the street
for a breath of autumn sun
buildings below.

His arrival realigned the deserted face
of a fruit vendor doing business near
the company steps: gleaming barrow,
apple, fall-strawberry, pear—

the last local ones of that year.
Pyramids held by green raffia and crêpe
were enough to dazzle concrete, or the sun,
but the man's thirst made the transaction.

A great apple, friend. He touched a bright
Macintosh until the dealer whipped it from sight
to show, in a conspiracy of air
and water, the long face of the true pear.

The vision needing no stronger evidence
than flooded through him as he bit into
the water-wall of the fruit, 20 cents
paid for the nectar-lanes trembling his mouth,

and while huge buildings weighed against the sun
and each man went back to his livelihood,
like morality entering an afternoon
the pear tasted good.

A Postcard from Don Giovanni

I don't envy
the people I make love to.
I don't think they do
either: themselves.
Is there something
they all have in common
about the eyes? the cut
of the mouth? Crafty.
They are all my pupils.
They have black pupils
(also they find me conceited,
wait for their loving chance
to refute me) and sharp
teeth for a soft mouth.
I have seen them watching
me even when they saw me
not looking, pretending
not to look: the seesaw
of deception between us.
Smiling they offer
terror-conundrums;
I hold the balance
for a little while.
Early one morning
I fear they will catch me
as I lie on a heap of them
trying to catch some sleep.
They will perform sex
miracles but not fool me;
soon it will begin to hurt.
They need to get rid of me
quite badly, I am alert
(yes) but the people I make love to
are intelligent. They have fox eyes
which take my mind off their superb
figures. I feel hot and quite afraid.

ii

Do not miss my rendezvous
with any of you.
I am on guard
against you, and handsome and hard.

This side of town
is on fire at the sight of my blue dressing-gown.
The old properties of codpiece and placket
make way before my English smoking-jacket.

I wish no one here.
No fantasies of friendship share
the line of ladies breathless at the top of every stair

waiting the old-fashioned creak
of my entry, too dazed and shivering to speak
to each other, each one mindless and unique.

The evening star
alone knows who they all are.
My wreathèd hearse
waits for me at the edge of the universe.

Do not miss my rendezvous
with any of you.
I am on guard
against you, and handsome and hard.

Waiting Song

Evil of him I will not hear
although he has left his features where
each pore and rub of the town
nuzzles the lip of my eiderdown.

I lie in bed, I think of him.
I listen to traffic. I should like to follow
him. I should like to follow
streets out of sight of my pillow
where the tramlines end and the lamps are dim.

        Evil is where we confess
        too little loneliness.
        My bed stretches its white plain
        miles and miles, beyond my pain
        and into my sleep. I have done
        all I can to make undone.
        Where the lamps are dim I shall sleep there
        alone ... I shall sleep there ...

        yes

but evil of him I will not hear.

The Beach Girl

A backache
in the sun: Andrea has come a long way

and she knows it, her body knows
how effortlessly

the orange-blossom chocolate-sundae limbs
reach out to a sea they've shimmied like

all day, all paid for.
She does not recall

the slip-up—after the show at the Astor
when she left her bag in a cab and the pills

were inside; Andrea says
the hell with them too often

and a girl can lose
her job in seconds any model knows.

Andrea's an innocent still. Her system trembles
to hold the new life there while she dozes,

wakes to the dead day. The sun's gone down,
shot of Miami for another turn,

the palms are fretful. She picks up
glasses, a sun-dried drugstore *Karamazov*,

her halter, and flicks an apple core to sea.
God knows then for a second by that ocean

Andrea stood monokinied, unaware
of one intent on making a devotion,

a landscape, a still life from her.

Like Nereids

I have little hope for these women.
You cannot ignore love, bathe
naked ten miles south of Atlantic City.
But look at that one
                        —did you anywhere?

salt in her black
hair. She looks
Jewish, perhaps they all are.
I think of their ringlets
uncoiled by the waves.

                        Forgive me.

They come here on consecutive fine
days, yet the sea
is granite today, the sky green
and unhealthy, each breast (twelve) a pumice stone.
I stop in the car to look at them
or fly down from Boston.

Duck Lunch

There is a man waiting,
a child shaping
a man from new snow;

three black pines,
cigar-shaped cones
touched with the snow like sugar,

and my winter picnic is lonely.
I have laid out a cloth on the snow
with salt butter and white rye
bread. From a thermos so
big I can hardly carry it
I produce a honey-coloured whole roast
duck and set it shining and steaming there
and eat it.

> The man is frozen
> in his tracks like
> a snowman.
> > The child takes
> > the scent in his nostrils and
> > comes over to say hello.
> —*Kid, wanna piecea*
> *duck?*

We dip our roasted fingers in the snow.

Star

She's rich, and keeps a crocodile
skin television on a ledge in her bathroom.

An elderly beech throws beech leaves at her window.
This is the country. She likes the views.

In town, in another country, she has a flat,
fame, a hairdresser. Here she does her hair

herself and rinses it off with an old kettle,
luxury water weaving down her back.

Then sets to sea alone on her white body
which light ripples, filtering through leaves.

Tawny the hair caught by soft water,
breast gentle, delta anemone ...

Mind in her eyes gone sleepy, hesitant
between a gold ring or aquamarine,

she sighs and switches on the television.
What smiles from the little window is herself.

Little Paul Klee Blues

The small clerks choose and sit on the coloured chairs.
Even the oldest does not give himself airs.

His beard comes drooping across the diagonal
Vestigially: no girls at his port of call.

No work either. Certainly no one cares;
Goes on tom-tiddling over the magic squares.

Backface, there are chunks of an ocean liner
And the little clerk foretells the rise of China.

His fury's musical; he stands at stare,
Catches that eastern angel unaware.

Someone will wing him over Asia soon.
Meanwhile the sirens siren at the moon.

Eheu, alack-a-day, oh what a pity.
The arrow looks like falling on the city.

For George Herbert

I am being reeled in by a peculiar
line, Lord. Oranges at my desk
turn this sunlight rancid and the fly that comes
over the windowsill is interested.
He brings the metaphor on angel wings
and treads like the devil—Lord what insistence of song!
The wind breathes past the curtains and into the poem.

An insistence of sun. I say the sun will hold
at least till the things in this room are rearranged
like clockwork with its falling, the distinction gone
between an object and its space; go carefully, sun,
but go. My room is ready, Lord:
vegetable, insect, I suppose man
ready to take up our revised relations,
trade hardness in for an evening's privacy.

For only in the dark are visions possible,
permitted by you. You must see
that. My capability
increases as I find it harder to write.
I'd like to suck the orange, swat the fly
poised on the paper as if to criticise
the lines he gave in moving up a hand's
corroded white, slash, and, by missing him,
turn these mystical fingers into thumbs.

Outside, with a world in motion and a wind
running the other way, who does not find
himself procrastinating? You prefer
gesture to symbol after so many years
of burlesque ritual, *pigges* and other bones,
submerged cathedrals, saints. The fly knows best
and is cast back into a second orbit,
an angel with a stutter. There's an image
appeals to the nonconforming two of us,
Lord! Truly our art is prophylactic.

Soon we shall enter into prayer together
but do not arrange history round my body
yet; show me the halo, not the dead
fact of the face inside it. I have been tricked
by the denseness of things, by my time and language and
the scavenging empiric eye which serves
the literal from memory's larder. Men stash the world
into their selves. Give back your balance, Lord!
Send your fruit in season.
Let me be brother to what's real, or angel,
not its victim as the fly is mine.

Postscript: The Lesson

As for poetry, bless
Tennyson for his line
'Now lies the earth all Danaë to the stars'
—a proper commitment
                    and George Herbert
who taught the Lord English
                              to make a man of Him
out of that knowledge;
                    bless the fliers,
the journeymen but not their journey
away from poetry
to the unplumbed regions—why plumb them?
'Solicit not thy thoughts with matters hid'
i.e. *Don't read the fine print* held no joy
for hungry Adam.

As for Adam, invent Eve:
the girl in the tree.
Consider how the tree holds but does not bruise the earth.
Is matched with forest. Loves it.
Well-read Apollo can't see the girl for the wood.
Grove-locked, he thrashes about
like a serpent
                    carving her name everywhere
so the wasted sap flows down the letterhead.

Face Apollo with the tree,
the taproot which divines the well of love
and spells it out, in Alighieri's leaves.

For Robert Duncan

When I have children
                    I should like them to keep
            the open measure of your poems

when after school
                    I see their feet
            point to the fields.

I want summer
                    to be their perspective,
            to keep time with them

and when they can read
                    I shall teach them to go out
            singing.

Easter Greetings for Samuel Beckett

Curds.

Meat.

A ditch under the sky of a sour country.

A naked man. A man newly fallen
into the ditch drunk or just dead.

April here and March only beginning!

Crow and fieldfare.
Slow crab in Atlantic
sleep, twofaced scare
crow, salmon jaw knit
with hooks, new
light on the cold
wind, clothes all going, things
petrified snatched from whiskey.

Earth, alive, smell, cloud yellowing

clouds move over
earth, earth over

men.

Piano

That night piano music,
high-toned, unnameable,
hammered away at my sleep.

I was so tired sleep was all there was
to me. But the dream flicker
took over: hundreds on thousands of keys
marionetting their way up their own strings.

They needed handling. Someone should have been there
to care for them, shape them a little,
see to it their energy became audible.

No one. Midnight—or was it the century?
gave back its zero echo. Stretched in fear,
my heart, my soft centre, fell away
leaving my hands empty but not released;
clenching still, knocked stupid by that night.

Clear morning opened the world like a statement.
Here is a bed, here's body: a niche regained
in daylight. Now, while the sound vanished

via the sun's touch, the piano was
more seen than heard and I thought Be visible, earth!
at a venture, too tired to face
dear body, worn heart with their dreams' music.

A Prayer for Intelligence

for Bernard Williams, 1929–2003

i

Mind, mind: in your small house
alive—things waver
from stuccoed fantasy to breezeblock
grey. When I call you
I hear echoes calling
selves I no longer want to
see but they remember me.
Worn ideas like bad
friends still blunder in and out without
thinking, no knowing them,
and their furniture, the old confusion, is worn.

ii

High on your nervy
pillar, clear
suntime, crystal air
becoming you—will you never
listen? will your ways change
subtly when at last you plummet and try
to unravel our lives? So high that your past
is beneath you; we dazzled ones
scratch at the surface
in search of a present—you, geometer,
survey it. If first name
terms offend you, if understanding
you at all is unlikely, may unlikeness be
belief received up there like a prayer from sea
level. Credible ghost, your descent
is desperate; fall and fill us; our plans miscarry.

Elizabeth in the Shallows

Elizabeth floats on sleep: a leaf,
a procession of leaves floating on the glass
because she pressed her bed against the window.
Car beams level her face. Trees go by.

Who knows what nature is? A bed
beaten into another kind of landscape?
A woman going swimming with the leaves?
If she woke up she'd say it was a feeling.

Night comes to an arrangement with all
who want it to be dark so faces blur
into limbs. People who work at night
carry themselves differently. Elizabeth,

you are a city state between scrub and sea.
The pine forests are deep in their second growth.
The sea looks dark from the river mouth
but phosphorus works at it: you see it glinting.

Elizabeth's eyes shelter inside her skull.
Industrial debris means no more to her
than stardust. Someone's cleaned up the river.
The town's red glare comes between her and the stars.

She is cast off from desire now. Her name,
covertly linked with the city and the sea,
has gone to sleep with her but the telephone
still grips itself like a conch beside her bed.

Anyone might call her! anyone wired
to everyone else—she is like everyone else
now because she's asleep; anyone draw
the wires tightly together, make her his...

but no one's at work in the forest except old fears
of fire and pursuit hunting each other in dreams,
the shadows levelling where Elizabeth's
dawn carves birds and leaves out of her trees.

Nights tender incident, their everyday
fires and murder—if sirens wail
near her all she does is tremble a little,
turn them back into wolves, sirens, a child.

Soon she will wake and reassess the city
with her own eyes, put on its clothes
if she wants to; if not, another night
brushing against windows will go to ground.

March Letters

The year was bitter:
catkin, pussy willow, had a time of it
            to lick the starry
            nights and their black woods wired by frost.

Here the sun failed
early; dogwood flowers struck the coppice
            later than anyone we knew could remember.
            By the last

letter you sent
from England, where of course lilacs danced about
            and the cuckoo sang in contractions,
            I'd say we compared springs.

No coincidence,
your first going came in with the cold.
            Love couldn't rise with sap there was so little
            of either: my trees were motionless

and frozen, yours
brought on into spring by the mild damp.
            Formally, I sent love,
            I felt our marriage widen.

We'd been happy enough
I thought. You wrote your father had died in Florida
            and was coming home by air.
            His rich body straddled the ocean between us,

a millionaire migratory ghost
sharpening the distance. My ill nature
            knew you'd be 'tied at home' a bit longer.
            You were thinking me out.

Replying, I still grew hope
in our garden; that bitter year a light touch
            beckoned you, as if its phrases were just stepping
            delicately as people must in cold weather.

The Outlook Is Fair Only

Rush hour:
a five o'clock downpour slows traffic
and muddies the sky beyond our apartment.
One by one
people turn headlights on.
You and I take our drinks over to the window.

There is little to sing about
but if you forget tyres and brakes squealing,
the golden beams are pretty enough in their way.
Take them from this angle. They might be pilgrims
thrusting candles before the shrine
of saint somebody
or even night fishermen in the Mediterranean.

Were I a child
(also, at this hour, a little high)
I'd scratch the whole scene out with naïve venom.
You would be startled
at the force of my dislike for our lives.
You'd compare them with
the spent machinery thickening underneath.

There are children enough.
Next door one of them is coupling tractors
furiously. He wants to father
an Ajax of an earth-mover.
Soon we will put him to bed
and read him two stories:
one about fire engines
and one about a pig with a steam yacht.

Poor one,
the glistening tarmac mirrors your unrest.
I did not mean it I say like a clumsy child.
I'll give you a whiskey kiss.
It is only people driving home from work
who claim me.

Jealousy Weather

Clouds: a low ceiling
for ten miles until South Mountain
liberates blue again to make the horizon.
I miss you, would swap words for a wind
to blow it all away and bring you
home. No one knows where you've gone.

I build a city
scheming under a tent of energy,
corrupt and choked by traffic, yet alive, living
on force—the millions
unable to bear or keep their hands off each other—

and put you there.
Not even neon defeats you;
your grownup purpose held with a child's intentness,
your absurd prettiness trailing
a list of addresses (I supply the names),
you tackle each street,

each apartment and leave looking so happy
I do not recognise you. Believe me, this
poison's the right fruit for jealousy weather:
cloud bank on cloud,
earth giving men little room to manoeuvre
but smug in its expectation of rain.

Smoke Curls

from a cup of coffee held in one hand
and a cigarette alive between fingers of the other.
The cup has a charred rim
and the cigarette two green bands and underneath
a word—*Salem*—written in green letters.
There is an argument floating about the two scents:
the prinking tobacco scent and the scent of coffee
black as a universe with no stars.

Necessarily a man is in the middle
of the fragrances, intent on
feeding first one then the other into his body.
His concentration has an eye for detail
but he'd like smoke to obscure and coffee drown him.

The Way Ahead

Descending cripples me. I show my new/
old love the stairs neither of us will admit
finding or wanting to find oh ten years
now though we knew the answer lay down there.
I'd say they're real ones (running into blind
alleys of meaning: what we meant to each other
always made our words come close to tears)
but she (as you do) tells me time out of mind
second thoughts are my second nature. Soon
like Wenceslas' page I'll tag whom now I call *you*
down the cold stone. My flesh crawls. Maybe
the stairs are crawling in their cantilevered
way to a place marked out for injury,
injustice, tortured and torturer's collusion.

The Words

I want the words to light on your shoulder
like a hand: touch but not take hold.

You understand they are no more than a gesture
between us and I have tuned my voice so low

no one else shall hear them: they are just for you.
Do not mistake them for intimacy however.

We are a long way off still—we have
a long way to go—the words may contain

an immoderate danger: words are so dangerous.
But if we are careful, if we do not make trouble

between us we shall learn to give them a name.

from *An Imagined Life*

Each time the tide comes in I'll marry you
again, Sorrowful. Wait till the moon lies down,
Sorrowful. We laugh ourselves to sleep
with a pint of applejack. Tomorrow morning,

what if the ocean has withdrawn forever
and the sea serpents come tumbling round the house
for care and cookies? Come close to me.
Turn over, then. Treat the poor monsters kindly.

Blue Café

A third-storey window,
no light behind you,
rain on the streets below,

so you look down once
in case and then stop
and look down again

into the lit window
of the last café in the street,
in case there are messages

caught by the thock and chime
of penny machines: *Come down,*
I may not be waiting but come.

The scene rearranges
itself into a face.

White plates rudely
slapped on Formica tables:
features in Morse.

No news from nature
except rain and insomnia.

I watch you
beyond midnight,

safe though my heart
is outdoors.

The one gesture
of a TV aerial

numbs me: I need food,
warmth and a little grandeur.

You are distant, cold
as a pigeon in winter sleep.

In a time of eyes
you are the only
blank for me to write on.

Fifteen

When Ruth Ellis was hanged Hope minor,
to the black embarrassment of Hope ma,
suffered a hard-on then bragged about it.
We noticed the tell-tale bulge at Boys' Breakfast—
powdered egg and tinned tomatoes on toast—
but happily m'tutor was almost blind.
Chastened, out of respect for his bro,
Hope whispered how it sprung at 8 a.m.
precisely: not his fault; a bolt from the blue.
After a hymn and the usual announcements
he made his way with the rest of us to the rears.

Twenty-Eight

The women start at your toes
and work upward: they
profit from your modesty and confusion.
But your sweet self is alas
only partly at issue, scraps
of scholarship betray your notions by
footnote, how little you remember!
Your bed is a terminus
where lonely unaccomplished lovers meet
not knowing where they are going but
certain that spring has misfired, their summery
confidence frozen into an attitude.
Poor ghosts, they are ripe for treachery
and get it. Above their heads, on Venus Mountain,
electric cells stir in the teleprinters
and burgeon, terrible directives
in sealed orders strip the summer night
bare for them, fantastic girlie police
give them a going over
                    —the sexual *Schrecklichkeit*
where you came in. For neither you nor your lost
shadows have violence left to handle the cocksure
Dionysian weapons wielded by your nights
of failure, the illusions disillusion brings
to trick you into putting out that white
truce, your pillow. Old loves reveal their faces
at daybreak. Like morning stars they shine,
brittle yet affectionate, knowing
their joke's on you. All over the day
the sun's prestige corners each dispute
last night gave rise to; the sun goes down
visibly on your stupor and relief.
                              If you can turn
the light to account your situation's godlike.
Command a temple: it fills
space with its rightness; at your whim the women come
begging in mid-sentence; ask a stone
for bread and the mountains are agog with corn
breast high and swaying. Your pastoral
tastes go perfectly with the latest and best

gadgets: rainmakers, cloud-dispersers, taped
decks of your own immortal music, clock-
work fountains that fix your drink or gently lave
the feet of your marble statues. Love, you say,
has done it. Starry
eyes, do you really think so? trust the women
whose contours always come between you and the sun,
whose mouths only whisper the abracadabras
you gave them? When you lie you limit
yourself, your imagination becomes an Italian garden
no rose may enter and your sex gets dolled up like a French
courtier sitting around with nothing to do
except sniff at the girls on swings. Dare you make
the journey back from fantasy to feeling?
Literature hasn't, you argue, and politics
won't. Yet essential life describes a circle
round both and there, cutting capers, at the centre,
lies—can you see it?—you. It is time to turn home.

Aspects of a Novel

The house is not locked.
Everyone open the door. The latch is old-fashionedly
stiff and though we are not breaking we're entering.
Uncertainty, cold
as nightlight, follows us into the hall.

We have nothing to go on.
It is very dark until at one end a fire,
the remains of one, unravels the room a little.
Yes, it is home; we are
faced with all the trouble we started from.

The people who lived here so
long ago, were they our family exactly?
or was their fierce kindness built upon difficult
kindling, bad memories to do
with us, with whom we were in the first place?

Our hands make blind-
man gestures along what is left of the panel
for a switch. A bank of them yields one 40-watt
weakling. Grateful, though,
eyes begin to grab at the parcel of shadows.

Charming! A miniature
grandfather clock, four foot yet carved so delicately,
almost tripped us (take care of those tattered curtains
too, they hang by a thread).
But familiar? The effigies hold back, nonplussed.

One thing: at some point
we were rich. The peculiar smell which money
does not have but we find lurking, when money's gone,
everywhere's here.
Later we may coax a story from it.

To the left, a schoolroom:
much needed now but our hypothetical German
governess, Frl. Weber, treated 'like one of the family',
fled from our high jinks.
A Gothic disapproval doused her smile.

The library is wretched.
Louis Seize bindings prop Chippendale amputee
tables; kitchen girls of the last days, working for love,
sealed jam jars with vellum
torn from a coloured atlas of the world

(1712) and we
need bearings, or at least familiars without whom
self-discovery's mere sight-seeing, our daily quest
a boredom opiate—
books *curiosa* like the lavatories'

Edwardian daydream
of two-tone copper ducts and high mahogany
seats giving on bowls archly bordered with peonies.
Dare we think the modern
life sprang whole from minds these rooms gave rise to?

Echoes veto
the notion though much needs to be answered
here, in this house, now. The walls trickle,
a black mildew.
Origins cling to us like sexual pain.

* * *

The house is not locked.
Children open the door. We may generate our own
daylight now and read heraldic doodles
in the beams of dirt
sneaking through chinks their dossier on a world.

Still, it is cold.
There are no voices, no residue of women
who then sorrowing or sweeping or melted by
love brought us back
once and for all where we always were.

Confidence beckons.
Mercy, colossal, a figure from allegory
with the amber flesh of a Titian, deliquescent,
writes her name in dust.
Their mottoes wreathe our heads in ectoplasm.

Be careful. Only
a few eyes, a few chimes of the small grandfather clock
back were we hopeless, transfixed beyond thought of succour
in the empty hall
of a house whose skeleton is gone desire.

How much did happen
since. Arguments, stories that tell the beginning,
throw light on a psyche, only flicker till we know
their structures are
durable prophecies—like a door.

PART TWO
The Domino Hymn
Poems from Harefield

for Magdi Yacoub

Transplant

Behind our house
larch pine needles fallen on the road
were russet first and then November gold.
Ideograms from an Oriental script,

they fell uphill,
striving to move the mind from sight to sound
until the spare traffic of the byway
rolled them like newsprint into the soft macadam.

Soon, in mid-winter,
still they were there, caught by the road's black amber
come wind or rain, sign and syllable.
From the daily walk

of a torn heart I entered, breathless,
to find myself reflected in the eye
of your anxiety. I said it was nothing
and thought aloud that Wales was like Japan,

or like a portrayed Japan: the broken
light of the offshore islands; the sky's compliance
weaving colourwash hills back into cloud;
the lone larch with one bird perched in it

from our antique scroll with the pretty, illegible text.
That autumn we fought
illness together until an imagined heart
took wing to fall and flicker with the leaves

quite happily, as if it were nothing of substance.
Who told it to? Things turned
right for the old one but, heart, who'd cut the larch
down for the view so he could keep the picture?

Celebrate

the crab apple
tree at the hospital
window. It waits our millennial

eclipse which then, at eleven
eleven, arrives with old-fashioned, Newtonian
politeness, precision,
the patch of blue above the television

zapped. In late summer
the lozengy apples find themselves in clover,
resources thrown at them to bring endeavour

to cardiac wards, to all of us waiting
our change of heart. The brief darkening
switches the birds off, turns yellow and red to purple,
purple to grey: an Atlantic hospital

in colours at once ponderous and hopeful.
As if to compensate, each of us is given
a miniature dawn, an initiative of heaven,
while minute by minute all the apples return

to post, their aura like a prescribed courage,
a chaos physics lesson, a Chardin painting,
a lucky break in the clouds, a turn of the page
and, punctually, the birds begin to sing.

The Squall

At one a.m. the BBC World Service
clocks on like a bedside whisper, not to disturb
the other patients. Nights are so quiet
we might be at sea and not this hospital,
floating on a chosen soporific
or anchored by our drips of Dopamine.
The night nurses have slept most of the day.
Laundered, alert among monitors,
they nibble biscuits and plot shore leave.
Then, as if to fulfil them, the storm warning.
Bleepers go off; a VDU's changed pitch,
a cry in the night or croak from an iron lung
brings all hands on deck fit for inspection.
Lights come on, patient sleepers wake
from semi-dreams of the death of a likely donor
or dawn alert of car and helicopter
bearing our lives swaddled in salt, in ice,
hopeful but threatening.

              The false alarm
ebbs quickly. We sink, relieved and sorry,
back on the pillows to the litany
of news from nowhere: Sri Lanka, Timor, Belfast;
a nowhere irredeemably Balkanised:
elections, GM dinners, ethnic cleansing,
ethical foreign policy, global warming,
post-Cold War synergies and soccer violence.
A few miles to the south lies Pinochet.
Monika, from Kenya, brings the world's
most beautiful hands and wrists to wave goodnight.
We drift towards sleep again in our subsidised cradles,
the radio a lullaby of disaster.

Harvest

All day helicopters—
loud sci-fi moths—weave and blunder
about in the mad way of the self-important.
Something is going on, Someone coming
or going. The TV is snowstorm,
the papers not yet arrived
and now, on an evening of cumulonimbus
leaned on by sunlight, burdened, luminescent,
bad news: a rail smash with thirty dead,
a superstore turned into a mortuary,
the wreathed furtive smile of a survivor.
We say our Dreadfuls and fail to meet
each other's eyes, eyes facing the screen,
each iris a well of anticipation.

Local

Shrub scrub
between Radiography
and where nurses live;

our small sub-
wood: stage flat with two or three
beech, one silvery

birch, holly and laurel and then
the fox-mangy lawn
beyond Outpatients—we thrive

on natural scraps:
slivers, like these;
like the halogen

mist of a moon
over Pharmacy;
the drowsy syrups

Tramadol, Zopiclone
which blind night ache,
or the borrowed sun

in our north-faced room
fooling the mind's eye and heart's care
that summer when

the E Ward woodpecker
did strut and take
light on his breast and burst into green fire.

Judgement

A man is falling
       to earth, to a linoleum
hospital floor. The bone cracks
       cleanly: shock kicks in with pain
postponed. The fall lasts
       point five of a second, life
wavers but as things turn out the man is lamed
       for life only and walks through
his day on a stick. As death claims him
       on a date his life determines, the sealed nerves
and seared tendons which replaced the bone
       heal punctually and irrevocably.
According to scripture all the disassembled
       limbs will gather again and the poison-flow
seep into the ground in just the time
       it takes to say so, pain a bad translation
of joy into a language without vowels,
       and the bone they carried away in black plastic
will lodge itself anew in the man's frame
       to brace him, with the passage of his breathing,
wherever he falls, to earth or to the sky.

Cull

Elephant pelt
clouds not moving
behind Laundry's smoke stack this morning;
a snow melt

puddle from
last night's flurry—
half-hearted, like the year in its infancy;
the odd petroleum

jellified hospital
smell; the rainbow
reflection of oil on water at the window
and torn calendars tell

Harefield to change
shift. Cleaners come
and sweep the decorations from each room.
It is time to rearrange

lives: the tinsel
tree and the cards
will go to Africa while we await the roads'
bounty, the annual

Christmas crop ...
Our wise men
wash hands together before the operation
and glove up.

Fracture

Absence of leaves in July, for they built the windows
out of sight, in intensive care, where the wall meets the ceiling,
    but light throws
cinema leaves at the wall, at states of being

which flicker from here to there, from here to nowhere
when the wind moves the leaves and the leaves their shadows,
    over and over
the faces and the equipment—the dying, the living.

Third Day

Respirators sound like trout feeding
at night in some dream hatchery—no one there
to listen; our subaqueous world of care
is halfway blue—peaceful, unthreatening.

Spectacles pressed to the glass, our specialists
walk by to look us over and seem the same
until, mask-mouthed, they enter: clipboard lists
distinguish the paraphernalia from the name.

We are our medication, and the machines
programmed to meet an individual case
more than identity now. We may have been;
some may become again. We have no face

to lose, to look at, but it's pleasant here,
suspense suspended, nothing to be done
for the time being—time being our time won
to flail for birth again and fight for air.

Gift

for David Sylvester 1924–2001

A last summer
of life, or at least misgiving
that leaves will billow again for the great
eye. How they enfold
even a hand held high against the light
this bed side of a window—blue veins
with green gradations beyond them, an admonition of green
which only the sun on a white rose by a brick
wall undermines to tell a different story.

Or the cloud spell—we know clouds are drifting
out of sight, over the wall, above a chimney
stack smoking in June from the waste disposal,
but it's all drift, the green envelops
the rose with only a memory of sky.
Sap is the tide on which we have put to sea.
It mimics the back of the hand, veins streaking
their way to the heart.

And someone has put a Coke
bottle, the old wasp-waisted sort,
on the window ledge and stuck a rose in it.
Pink this time, the petals are blowsy and done.
Light through the bossed glass via the window
has cauterised the leaves: life no longer—
as we go down into green from the white bed—
desolate but an amiable opportunity.

The Domino Hymn

Who would believe it? they film
the whole procedure now
    from incision to stitching-up,
with nurses stanching the brow
    of the exhausted surgeon,
and put it out on TV:
    a green parcel revealing
red guts for all to see.

Arc bulbs and camera lights,
scalpel and microphone,
    the crew, anaesthetists' nerves
and an electric saw-bone
    that jars, briefly, the light
banter of people at work.
    All know the drill and have seen
the killing-field mistake.

An act more intimate
than sex, or defecation,
    is saved from vulgarity
by the professional elation
    of a few men and women
who complete it now and tear
    their masks off at the result
as if throwing hats in the air.

And the wrapped patient, he
is wheeled gently away;
    out of it still, not a person
yet but not meat on a tray
    either: a skull-white, inert,
oxygenated machine;
    a shadow in search of the light
where a man has been.

We live between consciousness
and sleep, fly autopilot—
    night walking, day drifting—
until the lights go out
    as almost they did for this one
who will soon reappear and find
    the operation persuaded
his cortex to change its mind.

As at daybreak the birds
of Ruislip and Hillingdon
    stir in hospital trees,
turn out, flutter in song
    and choir the cardiac team
to a fry-up, then to bed,
    the dawn chorus of data
begins to play in his head.

A-level maths; a Leibnitz text
fluffed in '64;
    two hostile leading articles
in the Sun *and leaving before*
    the Queen; not saying goodbye
to his spaniel; a shaft of pain
    like sunlight, and somehow welcome;
a petulant call for champagne.

And as the Pentatol ebbs,
slow tide from a landlocked shore,
    sparks of perception fly
where muddle imploded before,
    flare like a faulty connection
then cannon along the vein
    of this organism acquiring
an identity again.

What is the price of light
when dew forms on a sill
    the moment visitors come?
Was it her business to tell
    the doctors to leave me here
instead—should I write a letter
    and complain about the singing?
Why do they not bring water?

Windows: papery shades
or slats maybe—slats sound fine—
    filter new knowledge: the heart
that beats is no longer mine
    so logically it belongs
to someone else who they say
    (so in the future they tell me)
is lying a few feet away.

    A Domino. A man
died and his heart and lung
    helicoptered to shelter inside
the cavity of this young
    man who lent me his heart
in turn that January
    night of the operation
in two thousand AD.

Postscript: The Magus

for Scott Everitt 1979–2007

They have built a tent
to raise glasses in, beside X-Ray,
and the guest of honour is the retiring
surgeon. He looks puzzled.
It seems he prepared for his last operation
(in our country) and it was cancelled—
routine, to be sure, but tough
luck on the team's adrenalin.
Now he must smile unsmilingly
and suffer the kind and clumsy
verbal malpractice of our valediction.
He is out of scale: a transplant, an Egyptian.

The luminous amber eyes are also reflective;
the cranium, identikit Professor.
After a while he slips away
to check on a patient, a young man
whose Elvad—mechanically aided heart—
came to grief in the throes of loving
a girl from Deptford. My time is
up, he tells himself, yours yet to come,
and it will come if they get you a new heart
and they will, you know; I feel it;
I feel it in hands which may not work for you
now, but they are intuitive—
steeped in cunning and catastrophe.
Aloud: 'Live. Look after your mother. Say goodbye.'

Minoan

'Why should the catalpa
tree by this north
London lawn carry
the eye indiscriminately

one long arc south—
past Olympia, over the Barnes
reservoirs, tail fins
tilted still, jet stream florets

turning slowly into white flowers,
like the catalpa flowers at ground level—
to a Cretan village in nineteen seventy
three?' 'Easy;

we were born in wartime
by Baltic and Irish seas
and aircraft are summer now, sky
happy. Life is loaded

in favour of northerners,
our plastic dough, our temperate privations'—
'Erst kommt das Fressen, dann kommt die Moral'?—
'yeah, yeah, and the way the light goes on forever

but they ration the sun.'
'Ah but intimations
of sunlight alleviate mortality
and we kill to get our way not to appease

death. Look how fecund
the garden is: our pocket Amazonia
where the bee sucks and the fox walks
behind bin liners

banked by a new car.
Is it an alibi of leaf
and shadow that lets you swim in this green sea
with your clothes on, unbeatable

really: the rain your scent of skin
now as on the night we stayed near Chania
and wondered if foul Colonels
licensed lovers on a pebbly beach?'

'It is just the catalpa trees. They look like vines
or holidays when you drink at lunch.
Svakopigadia ... did we sleep there?
When I was a child we did not go to the sea

but trudged the mountains. I like tree-climbing
and feel reflection when I touch a tree
with my eyes shut. It is time to go
in and take your stuff and put your leg

up: you are dark and dangerous still
and risky but I do not want to risk you
yet ... I am growing cold.
Watch the Discovery Channel or Wild Life.'

PART THREE
Marches

for Drue Heinz

Was Judas's Cover Blown?

This is what I did when I didn't
do quite what they wanted always allowing
I'd got into the thing myself and the other matter
also. The real trouble (or so they hinted)
was I was selling them short on information
though having the time and in a sense the money
to go about getting both since both seemed necessary
to procure it. I was too conscientious. Looking back,
it seems that what was needed was a response
modified by but not at odds with such data
as they were able to give me from what was at hand.
That much is certain now. I should mention,
however, the pressures put on me at the time
to swallow my own misgivings and start out
objectively (in this respect my hands were tied)
by deciding which points were pretty well beyond doubt
and which open to question.

                              They were not un-
reasonable about it and reports were framed in such a way
as to offer me enough outs for the time being.
I was grateful for that. One needs breathing
space at times and this was one of them.
All the same the feeling was there and when I think
it over from time to time I tremble to think
what might have happened (Christ!) if it hadn't turned out
more or less as expected and there'd been no chance
to clear everything up and in the end
shed a little light on the whole business.

Funny Old Game

i

A meditation between *The Bill* and *Newsnight*:
Orestes was an interesting politician.
When the law said, 'Kill your mother', he obeyed
though his advisers told him he'd lose in the court of appeal.

When he lost, his advisers told him, 'We told you so'.
Still he ignored them and lobbied secretly
for a change in the law—a retrospective change at that—
by getting the Queen to exceed her constitutional

powers, so everyone thought. But it turned out
that Orestes, not everyone, certainly not his advisers,
had spotted that the Queen had the final say
in exceptional circumstances. Then he worked on public opinion.

If killing your mum after she'd killed your dad
isn't exceptional, Orestes argued, behind the scenes,
I'm a Lacedaemonian, a banana.
Everyone thought the Queen had thought this up

and, not for the first time, was more in touch
than her ministers. They cheered her to the sky
and throwing fiscal discipline to the wind,
built an entire city in her name.

ii

When you look back at the thing, three things stand out.
One: gender was more important
than people thought, or liked to think, at the time.
Everyone front of house except Orestes

was female: the victim, the entire court of appeal
(all three of them) and then, of course, the Queen.
Two: so was sex appeal. The court was hideous,
a fright to a woman; Clytemnestra

had been handsome, to be sure, but now quite terrifying;
the Queen was pretty and, sideways, beautiful.
Three: the hopelessness of the Opposition.
Hamlet not only sat on the fence but drew

attention to the fact by ranting on
and on about the pros and cons of the issue
and, worse, about the pros and cons of taking sides.
Everyone knew this could lead to civil war

with bodies all over the place instead of fireworks.
Sad. Still, as someone once said,
politics, a funny old game, always ends in tears.
Inflation, as you'd expect, did for the city,

and arrogance: the Queen exceeded her brief
once too often; the bewigged and fearful bitches
were bought off for a time and bided their time.
Blood, in the end, was spilt all over the carpet

and *Hamlet*, not *Oresteia*, is the play people pay to see.

Angela's Dream

I cannot do business with Bohrer.
I wonder if anyone can.
My Jewish friends call him a *schnorrer*.
He is a most worrying man.

He knows quite a lot about Hölder-
lin and, so people say, Kleist,
but he seems to give me the cold shoulder.
I don't think we'll ever get spliced.

My sister insists he's good-looking.
Really? He looks rather wild.
As for brains, you'd expect the top booking
from a Teuto-Hibernian child.

Will he dandle my seven grandchildren
or bury himself in *Merkur*?
Like Macbeth faced with wife, witch and cauldron
he has reservations, I'm sure.

I'd like to do business with Bohrer,
I admit. We shall just have to see.
To his Petrarch can I be a Laura?
Can Bohrer do business with me?

It might be quite fun to speak German
again after twenty five years.
Shall we just have a fling or a perman-
ent thing—do I care if he cares?

Will my girlfriends call me Frau Professor?
Will I ever see London again?
Campus life's a tremendous depressor
and Stanford's twelve hours in a plane.

Good grief, I've just woken beside him.
I am faced with a fait accompli
and find that I've gone and allied him
and Bohrer's done business with me.

Album

How hideous
our clothes were: flared trousers,
herbaceous-border shirts and seawrack ties
lapping forlornly on the shores of fashion.
For what seemed a century our styled hair
cradled our ears, as if such innocent,
intricate shells were digital, erectile,
on-or-off items not to be shown in public.
Here is a marriage in its infancy.
You were the only girl in the world of Fleet Street
as I zigzagged a path through the arena.
With Munich—then—a vaccine against trendy,
your knee-length pleated skirts and cashmere V-necks
still hold their own this quarter-century
gone grace-à-Dieu and your effortless, musical figure.
We married that winter. Look, our wedding breakfast
at Prunier with Cal and Caroline—
quasars whose pulse still beacons us from heaven,
from their black galaxy beyond the stars.
The restaurant's gone, like the Cunarder Queens
it copied. Then Vienna: the books and opera honeymoon;
the pilgrimage to Kirchstetten in a rudderless
taxi when my sextant was the sequence,
About the House, written in Audenstrasse
(the village christened it; he died the year before),
the fields and churches and *Autobahnen*
drawn without rhetoric and accurately.
Ormai nella tua Carinzia: our day train
from Vienna to Rome: shirtsleeves, rooftop dreams,
passionate and compassionate embraces
and always the certainty of coming home
wherever we found ourselves. We were. *We are.*

If, or rather whenever, I offended
(spilling the beans without thought, backward opinions),
I'd find myself adrift in a Baltic winter
with fourteen generations of Field Marshals
sharing the life raft and heading north.
Yesterday the doctor called you in—
'Your husband has months, maybe, to live

unless we get a heart and we may not get one'
(thank God for a brusque physician)—and yesterday
the Prime Minister, who fronted a college band
the year we married,
took personal charge of me and the NHS.
In spite or because of the news we're oddly contented:
hand-in-hand for love in a hospital
relict of the Thirties and TB
built near the sunlit gravel ponds
of rural Middlesex, at the end of a century—
a life? a marriage? We drink champagne,
gossip and cry and test our origins.

Fern

i

Only in the particular
can we learn grandeur
you tell me.
              At Casa Ecco
your scenery has been
a postcard visited
from Romans to the Edwardians
waiting their cataclysm in Picardy.
The ribbon lake was always ice-green,
embracing everything we see
and half a mile deep: a submarine
siren, though today the sun obliges,
between showers,
your Alps with a parsimony of snow.

ii

On our walk the articulate thing
was a fern, light as a bird's wing
torn off when the hungry buzzard came.
If you lean
sideways for a moment,
the meltwater lake appears through a green flame
and the tourist towns—
Bellagio, Cadenabbia, Como—
stand where flood was blocked by a moraine

iii

when one of the interglacial,
tentative, millennial,
metre-by-metre convulsions
did for it.
              The promenade cafés,
touching in frayed plush and Venetian glass,
serve steak-and-chips and lemony sorbets.
Comaschi pass

no judgement at the fragility of the sun's
reappearance.
Spring happens. Things go on.

iv

Up here we are nearly
beyond reach of the noise
of speedboats and motorbikes
carrying on like bees after hibernation.
Our silence has no tension;
noticing one way of talking
and each step walking
an anchor as our days
blow away in the wind.
                    I show you the cold
fist at the fern's centre;
the ram's horn curled so tightly,
with branches so feathery, like the world.
If devils dance in detail so do joys.

v

Chilly in the breeze now, it is time to turn
back to the villa.
                Going down
the grassed-over steps you point to the great scar
where, last autumn, a badger wounded your lawn.

Drive

Medley of horses by the motorway
untethered; the field surplus to transport
or agriculture. At this speed the horses look
like Travellers' horses beside a leftover wood
where smoke rising sketches a caravan.
As we flash by our road draws its own wake,
a joyful anarchy of second growth—
beechy and larchy shoots, scrub, militant bindweed
whose canker lilies, malign and beautiful,
have everything to play and nothing to pay for.
Two magpies land for luck, a third joins them
to squabble over the brains of a struck fox.
Unscrupulous nature reclaims the scar tissue
of the M54; soon we shall see Wales
take charge of the twilight, a swatch of sunset red
filter the cloudburst above Wolverhampton
as our windscreen wipers, moody with time delays,
hypnotise a landscape of special pleading.

Georgic

It is the late summer of agribusiness.
Stooks litter the field like giant quoits
arranged for a game whose rules remain uncertain.
The big-as-a-house machine which baled them
has gone, terminating partridges.
The farmer drives home to an evening's paperwork.

Tomorrow he will argue the veterinarian
question, committees commit him to decide
quotas, set-aside hectares, indices
of hygiene. Someone has taken the view
a scrofulous hedge, for the moment, may be spared.
Who knows but this one houses a rabid badger.

Tankers for milk, tankers for gasoline
in long flotillas float by the wheatfield's shore
and drift towards the centres of distribution.
Their barrel bodies reflect the late light
westward: through electric masts a harvest moon—
red gold, archaic—pulls the scene together.

The moon, unfazed by contemplation,
at nightfall will resume its usual silver,
dark draw a curtain over the black plastic
sheets on the silage, over the rubber tyres,
and in towns and cities near these fields young women
shimmer through crowded aisles with wire baskets of food.

Severn

The yellow gantry above a sad
scatter of poplar by the railway side
to heft containers: beautiful, haphazard,
in massed colours piled, rust-red, blue-grey
like old Levis or a fine Léger,
their raggedy labels, stencilled destinations
tell us our city will be dragged away

and be dispersed beyond archaeology
or tariffs; the yellow-clad
humanoid arms on wheels make slack of steel
and shunt the goods of an old economy
east to an ocean. Here, in a stacking yard,
a wrong turning taken, all at sea
in a small car with irritable instructions
whispered invisibly on the mobile,

we may escape in wonder at this tiered
luggage: loudspeakers and brake linings,
tins of emulsion, silent pneumatic drills
and two-by-four shelves for self-assembly
kitchens. Safe in a world of things,
hemmed in ourselves by metal, we try to find
the way out or, at least, a causeway
home in the certain knowledge that what kills

is certainty; signifying; failure to see
momentary slivers of occasion—
the golden crane, the silver-paper tree—
that surface momentarily in dreams
like metal-seeking light or like the sun's
waltz down some lost avenue of the mind.

Marches

Imagine a wood
in Wales, virtually in England
a mile away as crows who nest in it
fly. The wood is small and scruffy.
Sheep can get in; a cow from time to time
disrupts the undergrowth, the private life.
The wind makes the noise winds always make
                               in Wales
with one difference: it sounds like Ireland
when pulled from the west.
Laid up in London you weather yourself
against pain and pain's narrow horizon
by learning the wood by heart: from memory,
from articles on coppicing or fungi.
Imagine negotiating an overdraft
in a soft wind with rain, in late autumn,
to purchase a wood you are unlikely to wander.
Naturally the purchase is value–adding
as you live by the wood and mean to live
                              in the wood
forever, gifted to an environment.
But with memory's eye and almost dead centre
of the wood lies a pool, mud with water on it,
which hides like a lost coin the mind's secret:
to live, live, walking against a wind
in Wales, in the mind, that lets you live in Ireland.

Gardener's Tale

Dog rose, waif-and-stray
cluster of torn leaves with pinky grey
soft-tissue faces; escapee
from wildwood, vacant lot or motorway
embankment; wet petals at break of day;
dropped handkerchiefs from the *Rosaceae*'s proto-tree

filed among fossils now; little weaver
of thorns sharp enough to crown a saviour—
who dumped you in the yard beyond our gate?
June has gone by like a hidden river
and we felt the green gloom would go on forever
and suffocate us. Humboldt, the cat,

feints at a sunpatch, snakes under the fence
to a kingdom of cans and old sofas, making sense
of empty beer bottles and rubbish bags
which skirt a siding; then, at once
querying and questing, waits to pounce
on a blind vole and tear its flesh to rags.

It is time to dig deep and clean up
litter of generations who chose to stop
in this Welsh farmhouse one sly mile from England.
South-faced to give the sun a chance to soak
into the bones of the living, for summer's sake;
long-limbed; square on the hill and built to stand

in full valley view, proud and plain;
sometime a house of peacocks, Ty Bain
is our beginning for the end of life.
Grey slate and red-baked brick hang upon
oak of Montgomery—in Wales, Maldwyn:
a decent diet, like a country loaf.

The land needs clearing, colour. Forget
catalogues and garden centres. Let
the dog rose lope within the precinct. Sow
kingcup, wild garlic, poppy, marguerite
and tread the hazel cuttings underfoot
into the ground until the grasses grow.

A new neighbour owns dray horses
bred in the Black Country whose white faces
come alive with affection for our kind.
He prays they will bring home prizes
from the August fête though bereft of their old uses
dragging ale to the pub, coffins to church ground.

In the long light of summer you can work
through to an hour off midnight without break
but we live under the ascending flight
path of BA One-Thirteen to New York,
ever on cue to set the body clock
to a faint bee drone from twenty thousand feet

and welcome us to a meal about seven,
laughing, or not, at those whose ground is even.
High on hills westward, gorse relieves
green with chrome yellow coinage from heaven
and any moment midge- or impulse-driven
bats, not swallows, will scatter from the eaves.

Gardening bookshelves call us to the wild
(Mirabel Osler, Miriam Rothschild)
while we have earth to wrestle with and free
from cattle pens and concrete, barbed wire rolled
and lethal; and plans for burying an old
refrigerator under an apple tree.

And share creation always, from the small
menace of gastropods: slugs and snails who crawl
and slime their egress; the proliferating bat
protected by the law; from the architectural
wonder of wasp nests to this miracle:
Rosa canina and a favourite cat.

If big themes are tragic, happiness
blooms in small corners: sunlight on a dress
moving in from shadow; flood water; a call
to capture the unfolding sensuousness
of white nymphaeas or purple iris;
absurd pleasure at the steamy pile

of straw christened by horses and settling in
to rot by the compost heap, good as a win
at the races, and, best of all, the bright
certainty that in the end sins are forgiven
or rotted down themselves, season by season,
and we have laughter while we have the light.

Courrances

How odd they were
at that time to shun display
or showing off to the king;
to turn away
(and so near Paris)
from Gothic high-minded,
Baroque balletic
clatter, brouhaha
for the grey-green house
and think (for a moment
or a whole generation)
of light in a forest clearing
falling and rising
on the long canals
(which did not exist yet)
they knew would be there
after their names dwindled
to a text on the front door.

Quartet for Charlotte

Something is tip-toeing round this woman
and turning the lights off, one by one.
She is dying of a tumour in the brain.

Her body has become occupied territory,
Glioblastoma Grade Four the enemy
which they tried to cut down, like ivy,
or infiltrate with the usual ceremony
of radio, chemo, acupuncture, prayer,
counselling: all the appurtenances of care.
The little mothwing shade is still there
on the X-ray. It flutters delicately on the scan;
mortal knowledge in the mind of man.

Her childhood names translate as doll or flower.
Her children will read her diary of the disease.
Her death unfolds among the synapses
as if it could be lovely, like a flower.

She has come to what for two years she has known
she would come to. She wanted to know and be silent.
Motion went a couple of months ago
(a little remained in one hand,
enough to sustain life with), then system, then sight—
her husband watching while she lost the light—
and now, in a few hours, her breathing.
Knowledge pervades the room, a small sigh
or someone saying death is only a sigh
for comfort to lay a body without feeling
onto its other side, for courtesy.
The nurses move her,
draw on her courage by talking cheerfully.

Now the house has shrunk to one room,
the room to a bed and in bed the woman
who built a place of books, dogs, laughing
as refuge from the politics of the tribe.

Her sons drive up from Cork, down from Dublin;
her daughter is flying in from Tokyo
tonight. There is one more morning
for husband, sisters, brother, children, grandchildren
to move about the house quite noisily
on purpose: hearing's the last to go.
Her life is melting in the sun, like snow,
like blow she craves and they give her.

It is high summer in north County Kildare,
the edge of the pale. Tomorrow is Bastille Day
and people will murmur release or blessèd release.
James Egan's aisle of beech across the way
filters the late light of a fiery sunset
onto her bedroom wall. There's light left yet
between the Bog of Allen and Prosperous;
a smidgen of the earth clings to its daughter.
With everyone cheerful, everyone unhappy,

> *unhappily I write*
> *lines on your death knowing*
> *you are still alive.*

ii

Born Lutheran, in Breslau, with the priest:
'Will I see my father, Father?'

'Why not? We go back, not forward.
We have a past so why not make it a future?
While we're about it, if we are talking darkness,
are not Darwinians more fortunate than Christians?
I mean their hallelujahs cry for process,
the odd propulsion of the universe:
whatever it is that makes us move or moves us.
In my case it's a Him; for my poor, Mary.
Gas is more boring than the giant tortoise
even. I promise to come tomorrow.
I know I have interrupted *St Matthew Passion*.
Good to hear such music in your room.'

iii

Canals dream their way through Britain and Ireland.
At this season verges come alive
with stitchwort, campion, willowherb, montbretia.
In memory of the Sixties and Robertstown
when you went in for horse-drawn water ski-ing,
I walk the Shropshire–Montgomery's flowering footpath.
I want to leave the flowers where they are,
strew them about your beauty in my mind.

The Grand Canal lazed by
Portobello where you had your children.
You nursed them while their father played cards
with rugger pals, a turf fire gleaming
in the room and the air curtained with smoke
from that age of smoking. Far and away,
over the Squares, in spacetime—Merrion,
Pembroke, Fitzwilliam, rusty Georgian Dublin—,
delirious imperatives in Phoenix Park,
the post-Pill paradise and the ilex tree
waited. Chance meetings
in the Shelbourne Bar in 1967
shafted a few lives. The Powers biddy
sang to herself in French in a chintz corner.
The Persian owned a nightclub with a piranha.

Our gang drank there one night with Haughey's mistress
and my friend Adrienne Ring whose liver failed
in Africa, years ago. Her father was de Valera's
bodyguard and when she was twelve Dev asked her name
in Irish. She bridled and launched the career
with the eyelashes—Sybil Connolly's best girl.
Gone where angels jar, one dark, one fair,
the two of you now, two beautiful girls in Ireland
walking beside a canal of memory
towards an Atlantic beyond memory.

iv

Your long road gone to Calvary, Plötzenzee
where they killed your father slowly
after the failure of the '44
Conspiracy. Sixty years, this July:
your July, your blessèd Bastille Day.
The Dark Ages: a slow cancer;
neither Armageddon nor *The Day of the Triffids*
but cellular life fast-forwarded
as if someone else were seizing the remote.

Days after your death
I rang your number to listen
to a heavenly, soft, Hiberno-Silesian
accent:

> *This is Caragh House.*
> *I am sorry we are out.*
> *Do leave a message.*

Flight

He practised writing
love on an envelope, pretending his hand traced
love on her shoulder—gently, not to wake her.

After a few tries
he signed the postcard With Love but his careless name
ran away at the border and over the hills

through the archway until
it smudged her address and spoiled the name of the country
where she lived with her husband and the things they owned.

Love, he remembered
saying—making and saying—is an idea
this turbulence can turn into a picture

you carry with you
for life long after the lives have reassembled
and the little sleep is over and all the names

you whispered are drawn
back into syllables breaking into one
flagrance: a name on a postcard and your name

signed with three Xs—
three birds flighting the hills of another country
beyond endearment or air traffic control,

beyond the white sigh
of waves moving on Dover or the Bering Sea,
or the moony upturned eyes of Saint Sebastian

borne by his arrows
to sleep in the arms of an altered heaven's embrace
in Antonello da Messina's version

on the other side
of a postmark pronounced *Drays-den* and sent with love.

Dingle

You imagine it clear
of automobiles, junk
like street furniture or
directional signs for
a couple of years still,
your road to an inlet
of western sea. Hear
the invisible thrum
of overhead wires when
a few birds gather
to perch there: they like
the feel of humanity's
message, claw to beak
and down and then up
to a mackerel sky.
A cold wind calling
from the east, behind you,
tears coat from the back
until stopped blind at
the two or three houses
of limewash and slate left
before land's end: the start
of a sea, a benign one,
you have no way of knowing
is going out or coming
quite slyly and stealthily
in. But walk on by,
fragmented, minding
your own memory
of love, which may not be
your lover's memory,
to a house where the road
ebbs and you feel sward
underfoot before ribbed
sand and the cormorant sea.
You will find how your heart
thumps as a telephone
rings, rings in that lost
parlour behind floral
curtains and an empty grate

for no one has turned up save
you, who came here oh
thirty years gone when tide
withdrew, bladderwrack burst
like sea grapes and a curlew
cried for Kerry behind you,
the sigh of far water before.
Shadowy, intricate
man, long shade of a woman:
indelible beings still,
yet blurred by the sea's habit
of leaving land to one side
and flowing back into sky,
birds the only creatures
to count on: is it some *we*
must fly here soon or two
others wishing a journey
one made with somebody
else? Which one? With whom?
Wires murmur exchange of
justice, justification:
the end of an argument
made in the last century
in a then poor country
while the Saudis struck
and hiked the price of oil.
Did you open things only
to peter out now by a bland
New Ireland touristic
shore with visitor centre
and car park full in summer,
the fuchsia that bled for you
a ghost in the old lane?
Cold wind but there's time
and hope because, listen,
a car is coming down
the road, as asked for.
Look, with love, at a woman
getting out of it in a black
shirt and whose black jeans
show off her white dog.
Throw a stick on the waves
for now you may be sure

the message will get through,
the answer phone in the sad
room bleep reassurance,
the car be first of many
packed with dogs and people
to take this road to the sea.
Your old life falls away
west, and all before you,
and slides towards Boston
as if you had it in mind
to walk, to drive on water.
You will defy an old
world's ending, let life flow
back where you left it,
circling a universe
that's only gas, like the sea,
and pray this iridescent
scaled mackerel belly
of sky may be storm's warning
broadcast: sea back to land,
traffic to trade, an accomplished
city of untidy human love
also, not this unanswerable
calm of your heart's erosion.

Finnish

Did the fifteenth-century carver
feel bad, bad in his mind,
a shame to neighbours? They, surely,
found him virtuous and kind

to customers, the crippled even,
and liked his magic. He'd cut a bird
or a pig out of chippings you gave him.
No surprise when the word

spread over the island and ended up
with the elders of St Michael's Kirk
at Finström, God's village on Åland.
Feeless, he set to work.

The little *uppstandne Kristus*
took days, months, more than a year.
Behind the pulpit, in a box like a coffin,
they seem to have hidden it. Unfair,

for the crucifix by the altar
(earlier) flows with blood
and grief from the hanged man:
the painted iron and wood

a machine to dispatch him slowly.
That carpenter hacked not carved.
Did our man feel in his belly
he would not be saved?

Flesh held no panic for him;
at least you got rid of its stain
with bloodshed and your body's
concentration on pain.

His *Kristus* has lowered eyelids,
hands working to bless.
The heart stops, as in terror.
What we fear is forgiveness.

So World,

woolgathering
minute fist of a planet,
marbled bluewhite and blue
in the moonshot photographs,
cranium-cradle, small
outpost of our corrupt
intelligence, maker and minder
of all we name our own;

make vivid the mile
of landscape dwelled by me;
alert who live in our house
to their possibility
each morning of mist and occasion;
see that your green
rises to meet the
savagery of our need

this Sunday, in the morning,
beneath the Berwyn hills;
in particular remember
all who have lived here, tamed
earthly antipathies, tilled
and cared for your wafer
skin; focus
the sun's eye inward to relieve our strain

and light in me, prisoner, a high
summery sense of what is apposite
to the shapes I conform to
freely: birds at one with tree and farmstead,
mind untying itself, an effortless river
A way a lone a last a loved a
long the!
                      Stepping well
to the side of its difficulty breathing,
love latched on me as I went home.

From Primrose Hill

an altercation of tower block
buildings with estuarine
sky. It is the turn
of our century, two hundred years

since William Blake
walked where we are standing,
and two thousand
from his conscript Lamb.

Sheep, certainly,
grazed in Regent's Park
at the last turn, over there
to the left of the Zoo,

and back in your car,
on audio-tape,
Milly Theale watched them
after the great physician

told her 'Live all you can,'
quick as she could. Money
delivered her heart's wish
but did for her friends.

Today you need money
to live hereabouts,
yet the knot of children
grappling with kites

or keening a little
in the February wind,
are constant, hail
from no specially defined

socio-economic
nursery: tracksuits, trainers,
anoraks and baseball
caps worn backward are quids

in the town over.
On foot, on scooters,
or hooded like novitiate
monks they weave in the shade

of a lofted kite
which merrily, merrily
on high blots out
the white winter sun,

the Post Office Tower—
renamed now: one
good building since World War Two—
and, just for a second,

a grey jet swimming lazily
along an upended Thames
like a great shark lunging
its way to Heathrow.

Imagine all the people
John Lennon sang,
X, when we were young.
And we do imagine them

now in the shape of children
sheltered from history
by post-Cold War
arrangement: the kids

born since the Wall came down.
They are the common
life of the city and one—
a grandchild—we hold in common.

He will reach our age
in the twenty fifties.
The way things are going
a gene-tapestry

will unravel for him
at fingertip touch
an archaeology of kin
with all mankind.

May he know where he stands
in the *demos* of DNA—
logged like the veins
and conduits of this place,

the ciphers, underground seams
opening now before us—;
know the random miracle
of being wired to the world.

Prayers like this
stop short in the wind,
in flux like traffic
seeping down the road

that abuts our hill
and dissolves in a delta
of Camden Town.
Nothing, we fear,

will change overmuch—
pray all the same.
The cerebellum
of a twelve year old

is pliable; soon
it may harden and beat
against the wall
of collective ill.

Desire's arrow,
like love or money,
burns for territory.
Not far from here

the Rolex killers
emptied their guns
into a family
for status seeking.

Footpads with mobiles
stalk Mercs and Beemers
to run to the Balkans.
Be clothed, we were taught,

in humility. The spires,
churches which jostle
for breathing space
on the Canaletto sleeve

of an old LP—
Haydn's 104th
blessed by Klemperer—
are obscured by Canary

Wharf and the NatWest
Tower; St Paul's,
almost as secular,
billows between them.

From this eminence,
with half-shut eyes,
we conjure the blurred blue
of pre-Roman London:

vegetative, boar-infested,
tribal as Ireland.
We have been here before,
will revert again.

But now a terrific
tea is in prospect:
the happy, diurnal
douceur de vivre.

We turn down a hill
which has seen it all;
where, in the dark years,
when we came in,

multitudes gathered
to watch London burning;
the virus we caught
ourselves over Dresden—

that ill reward
for the spatchcocked body
and carbon head
of the unknown civilian

who descends still with blazing
mercy for our kind
for Coronation fireworks, Jubilees, the 'new
millennial experience'—oh so

many years now! so many
people to contrive
a civilisation
and keep it alive.

Notes

Like most people who write poetry, I try to give shape to thought and please the eye as it travels down the page. But music means more to me; a poem starts with a tune and all these poems are written to be read aloud; or even muttered aloud: *sotto voce*. With the exception of 'Sixties' itself (2000), the elegy for Bernard Williams (2003), and 'Fifteen' (2003), all the poems in 'Part One. Sixties' were written between 1958 and 1970. Between 1970 and 1996 I wrote light or occasional verse only: 'Angela's Dream' and 'Funny Old Game' are recent examples. The latter is a response to an absurd request for a political memoir. At the turn of the century, and the new millennium, I spent nearly a year in hospital and underwent a heart transplant operation. 'Part Two. The Domino Hymn: Poems from Harefield' tells the tale and gives thanks for this miracle. A 'domino' transplant is when you receive a heart from a living donor who has in turn undergone a heart-and-lung replacement from a dead one. All the poems in 'Part Three. Marches' were written after the change of heart except 'Was Judas's Cover Blown?' (1966), which reads best beside the two light poems which follow and also 'Fern' (1996) and 'Finnish' (1997).

I hope the following notes are useful. They are in no way essential.

'Birthday Song' (1969). This is for Georgia (b. 1969), daughter of Tristram and Virginia Powell.

'Arabian' (1960). For Bronwen Astor.

'Baucis' (1963). Cf. Ovid, *Metamorphoses* Book 8.

'Lady Day' (1963). Lester Young's name for Billie Holiday: 'Heroes out of music born' (Sacheverell Sitwell).

'Father's Story' (1963). My own father was killed as a commando behind enemy lines in the Western Desert in 1942. Reading Stendhal in the bath is much more likely to prove the end of me. Cf. Marianne Moore: 'They fought the enemy, we fight / fat living and self-pity.'

'Postscript: History' (1968). A.H.: '...one or two odd things happened at that tea [with Hitler]. My mother and I were quite dirty because we'd come in an open car from Austria so we went to wash in his bathroom. Hitler's towels, I remember, had 'A.H.' embroidered on them. I always thought that was so strange, so unlike what you would expect from someone like that.' Deborah Devonshire in 2007, interviewed about the Mitford letters.

'Outside Biba's' (1968). Dedicated, nearly forty years after it was written, to Barbara Hulanicki.

'Oberland' (1960). Brienz is monosyllabic.

'For George Herbert' (1963). Twenty years before moving near to Montgomery, a celebration of the great poet born there. For '*pigges* and other bones' see Chaucer, General Prologue to *The Canterbury Tales*. He is describing the Pardoner.

'Postscript: The Lesson' (1966). For 'Solicit not thy thoughts with matters hid' see Milton, *Paradise Lost*, Book 8.

'Piano' (1970). For Malise Hore Ruthven.

'March Letters' (1966). As happened with 'Father's Story', critics of my first book took the poem too literally. The late father-in-law of my first marriage never visited Florida and was anything but a millionaire. There is a fine portrait of him in X. Bingley, *Bertie, May and Mrs Fish* (Harper-Collins, 2005). I like poems which read like archaeological traces of vanished novels.

'Fifteen' (2003). The execution of Ruth Ellis in 1955, the last woman hanged in England, caused sufficient public revulsion to help the abolitionist cause. Parliament ended the obscenity of capital punishment nine years later.

'Twenty-Eight' (1968). Paranoiac self-portrait. Cf. 'Dingle' (2003) for a less paranoiac self-portrait, aged sixty-three. '*Schrecklichkeit*': Hitler's declared policy of 'frightfulness' issued as a directive to the Luftwaffe in 1940.

'Aspects of a Novel' (1969). A poem about a house, Castlemartin, in Co. Kildare. Cf. 'Gardener's Tale' (2002), a poem about a house in Maldwyn, or Montgomeryshire. Originally preceded by a quotation from Conor Cruise O'Brien: 'Burke has a great respect for the social affection. He says "To love the little platoon to which we belong in society is the first, the germ, as it were, of public affection." And he did love his little platoon, which was, in fact, the Catholics of Ireland, although he by family accident had become a Protestant.' Burke is my political hero.

'Celebrate' (2000). The solar eclipse in question occurred on 11.8.99 at 11.11 a.m.

'The Squall' (2000). The National Health Service runs on acronyms. VDU is visual display unit; GM means genetically modified. The ex-Dictator of

Chile, Augusto Pinochet, was being held under house arrest nearby during my time at Harefield.

'The Domino Hymn' (2003). 'A-level maths' is poetic licence. I failed O-level maths, seven times, though I can count syllables, feet, etc. But each stanza starts with an 'A' or a 'W' for superstitious reasons. The title should be taken literally; the poem moves to an imaginary Church of England hymn tune.

'Minoan' (2002). *'Erst kommt das Fressen, ...'*: Brecht's phrase, translated by Auden as 'Grub first, then ethics.'

'Funny Old Game' (2000). This is for the theatrical producer, Thelma Holt.

'Angela's Dream' (2005). The 'g' in Angela is hard. Prof. Dr Karl-Heinz Bohrer is the editor of the German intellectual magazine *Merkur*. I overheard him saying, 'I cannot do business with Bohrer' at a dinner party and pointed out he had mastered a traditional English metre. He said, 'Show me.'

'Album' (2000). *'Ormai nella tua Carinzia'* comes from Montale, *Dora Markus*. A version in Robert Lowell's *Imitations* gives this as 'In your own Carinthia now'.

'Courrances' (2007). A great house near Paris. For Charles-Antoine de Nerçiat who took me there.

'Quartet for Charlotte' (2004). In memory of Charlotte von der Schulenburg, Mrs Thomas O'Connell (1940-2004). 'Powers' is a brand of Irish whiskey. Sybil Connolly was Ireland's leading couturier in the 1950s and 1960s. 'Canals dream their way through Britain and Ireland.' The small oil painting by Prunella Clough reproduced on the cover of this book is *Canal Side* (1983).

'Finnish' (1997). For George and Maria Embiricos. Åland is the Finnish island where they speak Swedish. It is pronounced 'Err-lund'.

'So World,' (2007). Adapted from a rejected poem, 'Easter 1969', in my first collection. The quotation in italics is the last sentence of *Finnegans Wake*. I used to live beside the Liffey, Joyce's Anna Livia Plurabelle.

'From Primrose Hill' (2002). Milly Theale is the 'dove' of Henry James's *The Wings of the Dove*. The X being addressed is my ex-wife Xandra Bingley. The twelve year old is our grandson, Heathcote Hore Ruthven, to whom the poem is dedicated.

Acknowledgements

Thanks are due to the editors of the following, in which some of the poems have appeared: *Agenda, The Atlantic Monthly, The Dublin Magazine, The Guardian, Gemini, The Irish Times, Isis, The Listener, Poetry (Chicago), The Spectator, The Sunday Telegraph, The Times Literary Supplement.*

'For George Herbert' was published as a Pym-Randall Press limited edition in Cambridge, Massachusetts in 1966. A second edition, to which 'Postscript: The Lesson' was added, was published by the Greville Press in 2006.

Agenda Editions and the Greville Press published two editions of Part Two of this book, 'The Domino Hymn: Poems from Harefield' in 2005 and 2006.

Other poems in this book previously published in separate limited editions by the Greville Press are: 'Aspects of a Novel', 'Dingle', 'From Primrose Hill', 'Gardener's Tale', and 'Quartet for Charlotte'.

Many of the poems in 'Part One. Sixties' appeared in *A Postcard from Don Giovanni* (Oxford University Press, 1972).

'Local' appears in *Signs and Humours: The Poetry of Medicine*, ed. Lavinia Greenlaw (Calouste Gulbenkian Foundation, 2007).

I would like to thank Christopher Reid, Roy Foster, Anthony Astbury, Daniel Farrell, Jane Amos and Lucy De Nardi for their help with the preparation of *Third Day*.